Box Trucking
Made Simple

The Fast Track Guide to Get Started in the Box Trucking Business

Cameron West

Contents

Introduction   1

1. Step 1: LL to the C   2

2. Step 2: Bank on it   6

3. Step 3: Boxed In   8

4. Step 4: Equipment   12

5. Step 5: The Road Ahead   14

6. Step 6: Getting Paid $$ 21

7. Step 7: The Wrap Up   25

8. One Last Thing   27

Introduction

If you're a beginner in the box trucking business, you're probably looking for a quick and easy guide to get you started on your new career. This book is intended to be just that a concise and straightforward guide that provides the first essential information you need to know to start your career in box trucking.

This book is not meant to be a comprehensive guide to trucking or box trucking. Instead, it's a quick reference guide that you can turn to when you need answers to specific questions or guidance on a particular topic. It's designed to be an easy-to-read resource that you can if you're just starting out in the industry.

So, if you're looking for a comprehensive guide to trucking, this may not be the book for you. But if you're looking for a quick and accessible reference guide that can help you navigate the world of box trucking, then you're in the right place. Let's get started!

Chapter One

Step 1: LL to the C

What is an LLC and why do I need one?

Starting an LLC (Limited Liability Company) can be important for your box trucking business for several reasons. Firstly, an LLC provides limited liability protection for its owners, meaning that the personal assets of the owners are typically protected from business debts and lawsuits. This is important because the trucking industry can be inherently risky, with accidents, damage to goods, and other unexpected events that can result in legal disputes and financial liabilities. By forming an LLC, the owners can shield their personal assets from these types of risks and potentially avoid financial ruin.

Having an LLC can make it easier to obtain financing for your box trucking business. Many lenders and investors prefer to work with LLCs because they are considered to be more stable and have more formalized business structures than sole proprietorships or partnerships. This can help you secure the capital you need to purchase trucks, hire drivers, and grow your business.

Forming an LLC can help enhance your box trucking business's credibility and professionalism. It shows that you have taken the time and effort to establish a formal legal structure for your business, which can give customers, vendors, and other business partners more confidence in your ability to deliver high-quality services and products.

There may be potential tax benefits associated with forming an LLC for your trucking business. LLCs are considered LLCs are classified as pass-through entities, which means that the profits and losses of the business are recorded on the owners' personal tax returns. This can result in tax savings compared to other types of business structures, such as corporations.

Starting an LLC for your box trucking business can provide several benefits, including limited liability protection, easier access to financing, enhanced credibility, and potential tax benefits. However, it's important to note that the exact advantages and requirements may vary depending on the state where you're operating and the specifics of your business. It's always a good idea to consult with a lawyer or a business formation service to ensure that you're making the best decision for your business.

How to start an LLC – Step by Step

- **Choose a name for your box truck LLC:** You'll need to select a name that's unique and not already in use by another business. You can check the availability of a name using your state's business name database.

- **Select a registered agent:** A registered agent is a person or business authorized to receive legal documents and other official communications on behalf of your LLC. You can hire a registered agent service or choose someone in your company to serve as the registered agent (don't use your home address).

- **File Articles of Organization:** This is the formal document that creates your LLC and provides information such as the company's name, address, registered agent, and management structure. You'll need to file Articles of Organization with the Secretary of State's office in the state where you'll be operating.

- **Obtain necessary permits and licenses:** Depending on the type of goods you'll be transporting; you may need to obtain permits and licenses from state and federal agencies. These may include a Commercial Driver's License (CDL) and a Motor Carrier Number (MC Number).

- **Obtain an Employer Identification Number (EIN):** An EIN is a unique identification number assigned to your business by the IRS. You'll need an EIN to open a business bank account, file tax returns, and hire employees.

- **Draft an Operating Agreement:** An operating agreement is a legal document that outlines how your LLC will be managed, including the roles and responsibilities of members, how profits and losses will be allocated, and the process for adding or removing members.

- **Register for state taxes:** Depending on the state where you're operating, you may need to register for state taxes such as sales tax, use tax, and withholding tax.

The process of starting an LLC for your box trucking company may vary slightly depending on the state where you'll be operating. It's always a good idea to consult with a lawyer or a business formation service to ensure that you're following all the necessary steps and requirements.

Key Takeaways

EIN Number - Obtaining an EIN (Employer Identification Number) for your box trucking business is a relatively simple process that can usually be completed online for free in just a few minutes.

To apply for an EIN online, you can visit the IRS website and navigate to the EIN application page. From there, you will need to provide basic information about your business, including its legal name, structure, address, and the name and Social Security number of the owner or responsible party.

Once you have submitted your application, you will receive your EIN immediately, and you can begin using it to conduct business and comply with tax and legal requirements.

It's important to note that obtaining an EIN is generally free of charge, and you do not need to pay a third-party service to obtain one on your behalf. While some companies may offer to obtain an EIN for you for a fee, there is no need to use these services, as the application process is straightforward and can be completed easily by most business owners.

Chapter Two

Step 2: Bank on it

O pening a business checking account is an important step in managing your finances as a small business owner. Not only does it help you keep your personal and business expenses separate, but it can also make it easier to track your income and expenses and ensure that you are following tax and legal requirements.

To open a business checking account for your box truck company, you will need to gather some important documents and information. This may include your business license, articles of incorporation or organization, your EIN (Employer Identification Number), and proof of identity for all account signers.

Once you have gathered the necessary documents and information, you can begin shopping around for a bank that offers business checking accounts that meet your needs. Look for a bank that offers low fees and convenient online and mobile banking options, as well as any other features that are important to you, such as ATM access or the ability to deposit checks remotely.

When you have chosen a bank, you can begin the application process for a business checking account. This may involve filling out an application form, providing documentation and information about your business, and meeting with a bank representative to discuss your needs and preferences.

After your application has been reviewed and approved, you will typically receive your account information and debit card in the mail within a few business days. You can then begin using your business checking account to manage your finances and keep your business running smoothly.

Chapter Three

Step 3: Boxed In

When it comes to selecting a box truck for over-the-road use, there are a few factors to consider, including reliability, length, fuel efficiency, cargo capacity, and comfort for the driver.

Renting vs. Leasing Pros and Cons:

Renting Pros:

Lower initial costs: Leasing a box truck typically requires a smaller down payment than buying one outright. This can make it easier to get started in the trucking business, especially if you don't have a lot of cash on hand.

Lower monthly payments: Leasing a box truck usually comes with lower monthly payments than financing a purchase. This can help you manage your cash flow and keep your business expenses under control.

No maintenance or repair costs: When you lease a box truck, the leasing company is typically responsible for maintenance and repairs. This can save you a lot of money in the long run, as maintenance and repair costs can add up quickly.

Ability to upgrade regularly: Leasing a box truck allows you to upgrade to a newer, more advanced model every few years. This can help you stay competitive and keep up with changes in the industry.

<u>**Renting Cons:**</u>

Limited flexibility: Leasing a box truck usually comes with strict mileage limits and other restrictions. This can limit your ability to use the truck as you see fit and may lead to additional fees if you exceed the limits.

No equity: When you lease a box truck, you don't own it outright. This means that you can't build equity in the truck, and you won't have any asset to sell or trade-in if you decide to leave the business.

Higher total cost: While leasing may have lower monthly payments, you'll likely end up paying more over the long run. This is because you'll be making payments for the entire lease term, which can be several years, and you won't have any equity to show for it.

Restrictions on customization: Leasing a box truck may come with restrictions on customizations and modifications. This can limit your ability to customize the truck to meet your specific needs and preferences.

<u>**Owning Pros:**</u>

More control: When you own a box truck, you have complete control over how you use it. There are no mileage limits or other restrictions, and you can customize the truck to meet your specific needs and preferences.

Equity: As you make payments on your box truck, you're building equity in the asset. This means that you have the option to sell the truck or use it as a trade-in if you decide to leave the business.

Potential cost savings: While owning a box truck may have higher upfront costs, you'll likely save money in the long run. This is because you won't be making payments for the entire life of the truck, and you'll have the option to sell it or trade it in when it's time for an upgrade.

Tax benefits: When you own a box truck, you may be able to take advantage of tax deductions for depreciation, maintenance, repairs, and other business expenses.

Owning Cons:

Higher upfront costs: Buying a box truck outright can be expensive, especially if you're just starting your business. You'll need to have enough cash on hand or be able to secure financing to make the purchase.

Maintenance and repair costs: When you own a box truck, you're responsible for all maintenance and repair costs. This can be a significant expense, especially if you have an older truck that requires frequent repairs.

Depreciation: Like any asset, a box truck will depreciate over time. This means that it will lose value as it gets older, which can impact your ability to sell it or trade it in for a newer model.

Potential for downtime: If your box truck breaks down or requires extensive repairs, it can lead to downtime for your business. This can impact your ability to meet customer demands and generate income.

Ultimately, the decision to own or lease a box truck for your business will depend on your specific needs, goals, and financial situation. It's important to carefully consider the pros and cons of each option before deciding.

Box Trucks Worth Considering for Your Business

You, as the owner-operator, have the freedom to choose any type of box truck that suits your business needs. However, the following list includes a few trucks that are highly recommended for over-the-road box trucking.

Freightliner M2 106 Box Truck

A popular option for a box truck of at least 26ft long is the Freightliner M2 106. This truck is known for its durability and reliability, making it a great choice for long-distance hauling. It also offers excellent fuel efficiency, thanks to its aerodynamic design and advanced engine technology. The Freightliner M2 106 has a maximum payload capacity of around 33,000 pounds, which should be sufficient for most over-the-road hauling needs.

International MV Series

Another option to consider is the International MV Series. This truck is designed specifically for medium-duty applications, making it well-suited for box truck use. It offers a comfortable and spacious cab, along with advanced safety features and excellent fuel efficiency. The International MV Series has a maximum payload capacity of around 28,000 pounds, which should be more than enough for most over-the-road hauling needs.

Ideally you want a box truck that is at least 26ft in length, that has a lift gate, and air ride suspension.

A box truck that is at least 26ft in length can accommodate larger loads and is generally more efficient for over-the-road transportation. A lift gate can make it easier to load and unload heavy items without the need for additional equipment or manpower. Additionally, having an air ride suspension can provide a smoother ride for your cargo, which can help reduce the risk of damage during transportation. Overall, these features can improve the safety, efficiency, and effectiveness of your box trucking business.

Chapter Four

Step 4: Equipment

O nce you have determined the type of box truck that will best suit your needs, it's time to think about what equipment you'll need to ensure a smooth and efficient operation. Depending on the nature of your business, you may need specialized tools or equipment, such as pallet jacks, hand trucks, or moving blankets to secure your cargo. Keep in mind that having the right equipment can not only help you avoid damage to your cargo but can also minimize the risk of accidents and injuries during loading and unloading.

You should have on your box truck minimum:

- **Dolly**

- **Toolbox**

- **2 eTrack Load Bars**

- **2 Normal Load Bars (if you don't have a track)**

- **8 eTrack Straps**

- **A Solid Lock for the truck**

- **Pallet Jack (at least 5500lbs)**

- **Pallet Jack Stand**

- **Tire chains and snow tires (especially if you are driving in the Northern states)**

While this is not an exhaustive list, these items are essential for any box truck driver. Of course, as you gain experience, you may find it necessary to add additional equipment to this list. However, the following items represent the basic standard that you should have on your box truck.

In addition to these essential pieces of equipment, there are a few optional items that can make your life on the road more comfortable and convenient. For example, a mini-fridge or cooler can be useful for storing food and drinks, and a power inverter can allow you to charge your phone or other devices while on the go. A comfortable and supportive seat can also make a big difference on long drives, as can a good sound system or audio books to help pass the time. Ultimately, the equipment you choose to carry will depend on your specific needs and preferences, as well as the type of cargo you will be hauling.

Chapter Five

Step 5: The Road Ahead

Dot and MC Numbers

After completing the necessary steps of obtaining a business name and an Employer Identification Number (EIN), the next step is to register for a DOT and MC number. This can be done at FMCSA.com. While the process of registration is relatively straightforward, it can take some time to get the numbers activated.

To begin the MC number registration, a payment of $300 is required. Upon submitting the application, there is a 60-day window to complete and submit all other required documents; failure to do so will result in the suspension of the numbers and the need to reactivate them. It is important to note that DOT and MC information is public, and once registered, businesses can expect to receive numerous calls and emails offering additional services.

It is important to keep in mind that the FMCSA will not use email, phone, or text to contact you with registration information. Any messages you receive may be from third-party providers who could charge a fee for their services. However, the FMCSA will send letters through the mail outlining what is needed to complete the registration process, including a phone number to verify everything is correct before final processing and activation. You may also receive reminders through the mail about outstanding items and deadlines if you are not yet active.

Additionally, it's crucial to ensure that the business name, EIN, and DOT/MC numbers match precisely. If you made a mistake obtaining the EIN, it's easy to request a new one. However, if you need to change the company name or EIN for the DOT/MC registration, you can do so through the FMCSA Portal, which you'll receive information on accessing after submitting the DOT/MC application. It's important to note that changing the company name incurs a $15 charge.

BOC-3

BOC-3 stands for "Blanket of Coverage Form 3," and it is a filing that must be submitted to the Federal Motor Carrier Safety Administration (FMCSA) by all interstate motor carriers operating in the United States. BOC-3 is also known as "Designation of Agents for Service of Process," which means it designates an agent that will accept legal documents on behalf of your company in case you are sued or summoned to court.

In other words, BOC-3 is a way for the government to ensure that motor carriers have a legal representative available to receive any legal documents on their behalf if they are unable to be contacted directly. This requirement applies to all motor carriers, including owner-operators, leased operators, and carriers operating under their own authority.

If you have an over-the-road box truck business that operates in multiple states, you will need to file a BOC-3 form with the FMCSA. Failing to do so can result in fines, penalties, and even a suspension of your operating authority. BOC-3 filing is mandatory for obtaining and maintaining your Motor Carrier (MC) number, which is required to transport freight across state lines.

To file for BOC-3, you must first obtain a USDOT number from the FMCSA. Once you have your USDOT number, you can file for BOC-3 online or by mail. The filing fee is $50, and it is valid for two years.

UCR

UCR is a federal registration program for motor carriers, brokers, and freight forwarders operating in the United States. UCR is administered by the UCR Board, which is a group of state and federal officials who work together to establish and implement the program. The goal of UCR is to ensure that motor carriers and other transportation companies are registered and compliant with safety and financial regulations.

If you have an over-the-road box truck business that operates in the United States, you will need to register for UCR. UCR registration is mandatory for all interstate carriers, and failure to register can result in fines and penalties. The UCR fees are based on the number of vehicles that your business operates, and the fees vary by state.

To register for UCR, you must first determine the number of vehicles that your business operates and the state in which you are based. Once you have this information, you can register online through the UCR website or by mail. The registration fee must be paid annually, and the deadline for registration is December 31st of each year.

Dot Physical

A DOT physical is a medical examination that is required by the Department of Transportation (DOT) for commercial drivers who operate vehicles that weigh more than 10,000 pounds or transport hazardous materials. The purpose of the DOT physical is to ensure that drivers are physically capable of operating a commercial motor vehicle safely.

As a truck driver, you will need to obtain a DOT physical to ensure that you meet the physical and medical requirements set forth by the DOT. These requirements include vision, hearing, blood pressure, and overall health. The DOT physical is typically valid for two years, after which you will need to obtain another physical examination to maintain your certification.

To obtain a DOT physical, you will need to visit a certified medical examiner who has been approved by the Federal Motor Carrier Safety Administration (FMCSA). You can find a certified medical examiner through the National Registry of Certified Medical Examiners (NRCME) website. The examiner will perform a physical examination, which may include vision and hearing tests, blood pressure checks, and a review of your medical history. The examiner will then complete a Medical Examination Report and issue a Medical Examiner's Certificate if you meet the DOT physical requirements.

It is important to note that failing to obtain and maintain a valid DOT physical can result in fines, penalties, and even a suspension of your commercial driver's license. As such, it is important to schedule and complete your DOT physical in a timely manner to ensure that you remain compliant with DOT regulations.

NOTE:

If you are either a driver or an owner operating a commercial motor vehicle that weighs over 10,000 pounds or transports hazardous materials, obtaining a DOT physical is mandatory. However, if you are an owner-operator who does not have a commercial driver's license (CDL), you have the option to take the non-CDL DOT physical.

Insurance

Insuring your OTR box truck for business purposes involves several steps. The first step is to determine what type of insurance coverage you need. Liability insurance is mandatory for all commercial vehicles, but you may also want to consider additional coverage such as collision insurance, comprehensive insurance, or cargo insurance depending on the nature of your business.

Next, you'll need to gather information about your truck, including its make and model, the year it was manufactured, and its vehicle identification number (VIN). You'll also need to provide information about the drivers who will be operating the truck, including their names, ages, and driving histories.

Once you have this information, you can start shopping for insurance quotes. It's a good idea to get quotes from multiple insurance providers to compare rates and coverage options. When you're reviewing quotes, make sure to pay attention to the deductible amounts, coverage limits, and any exclusions or restrictions that may apply.

Once you've selected an insurance provider and policy, you'll need to provide them with the necessary documentation and pay the premium. Depending on the insurance company, you may be able to do this online or over the phone.

It's important to note that commercial truck insurance can be complex, so it's a good idea to work with an experienced insurance agent who can help you navigate the process and ensure that you have the coverage you need. They can also help you understand the different types of insurance available and recommend options that are best suited for your business.

- **Typically, the insurance policy coverage for your box truck should include (example):**

- **Auto Liability Insurance of $1,000,000 or more.**

- **Motor Truck Cargo insurance of $100,000 or more.**

- **Commercial General Liability Insurance of $100,000 per occurrence and $2,000,000 in the aggregate.**

- **Workers compensation insurance in state company operates.**

- **Employer Liability of $100,000 per occurrence or more.**

Drivers Qualification File

A driver qualification file is a set of documents and records that trucking companies are required to maintain for each of their drivers. These files are an important part of the compliance process and are used to ensure that drivers meet all the necessary qualifications and regulations.

The driver qualification file typically includes documents such as the driver's application for employment, driving record, medical examiner's certificate, and proof of completed training. It may also include additional documents such as a copy of the driver's commercial driver's license (CDL), drug and alcohol test results, and road test evaluation.

The purpose of the driver qualification file is to ensure that drivers meet all the necessary qualifications and regulations, such as age requirements, experience requirements, and physical fitness requirements. It also helps ensure that drivers have completed the necessary training and have a clean driving record.

Trucking companies are required to maintain driver qualification files for all of their drivers, and the files must be updated regularly to ensure that they are accurate and up to date. In the event of an audit or inspection, the driver qualification file will be reviewed to ensure that all necessary documentation is present, and that the driver meets all the necessary qualifications.

Note:

As a trucking business owner who is also a driver, you will need to create a driver qualification file for yourself. The process of creating a driver qualification file is similar to creating files for your other drivers, but you will be gathering and organizing the necessary documentation for your own qualifications and compliance with FMCSA regulations.

To begin, you will need to obtain your own application for employment, driving record, medical examiner's certificate, and proof of completed training. You may also need to provide documentation such as your commercial driver's license (CDL) and any drug and alcohol testing records. You can obtain these documents from various sources, such as your previous employers, medical examiners, and the DOT.

Once you have gathered all of the necessary documents, you will need to organize them into a driver qualification file for yourself. This file should be kept separate from the files of your other drivers and should be updated regularly to ensure that it remains accurate and up to date.

It's important to ensure that your driver qualification file is compliant with all FMCSA regulations. This includes ensuring that your medical certification is current and that you meet all of the necessary qualifications for driving a commercial motor vehicle.

Chapter Six

Step 6: Getting Paid $$

D ispatchers

As a trucking business owner, you may have heard of dispatchers and wondered what their role is in your business. Dispatchers are individuals who are responsible for coordinating and organizing the movement of freight and goods from one location to another. They act as a bridge between the drivers and the customers, ensuring that the delivery process runs smoothly and efficiently.

Dispatchers are essential to your trucking business because they help you to manage the logistics of your operations. They work closely with your drivers to ensure that they are on schedule, and they keep track of the delivery status of each load. Dispatchers also help to maintain communication between you and your customers, ensuring that they are satisfied with your services and that their needs are being met.

To connect and contact dispatchers, you can either hire them as employees or outsource the service from a dispatch company. You can also search for dispatchers through online job boards or industry associations. When hiring dispatchers, it is essential to ensure that they have the necessary experience and qualifications to perform the job effectively. They should have excellent communication skills, be able to multitask and work well under pressure.

Note:

As a truck driver, obtaining your first load from a dispatcher may seem daunting at first, but the process is relatively straightforward. The first step is to establish communication with the dispatcher, either through a phone call, email or a messaging platform. You will need to provide some basic information about your truck, such as the type, size, and capacity, as well as your availability and location.

Once the dispatcher has this information, they will start looking for available loads that match your specifications. They will consider factors such as the distance, weight, and delivery timeline when selecting the right load for you. Once they have identified a suitable load, they will contact you with the details and provide you with all the necessary information, such as the pickup and delivery locations, contact details for the customer, and any special instructions.

At this point, you will need to confirm that you are available and willing to take on the load. You should also ask any questions you have to clarify any uncertainties, such as the expected delivery timeline or any special instructions you need to follow. Once you are satisfied with the information, you will need to accept the load, and the dispatcher will provide you with all the necessary documentation, such as the bill of lading and load confirmation.

Locating Dispatchers

There are several ways to locate and contact dispatching companies. One way is to conduct an online search using keywords such as "trucking dispatching companies" or "freight dispatching services." This search will provide you with a list of companies that offer dispatching services for trucking businesses.

Another way is to check with industry associations such as the American Trucking Associations (ATA) or the Owner-Operator Independent Drivers

Association (OOIDA). These associations often have directories of dispatching companies that specialize in providing services to the trucking industry.

When choosing a dispatching company, it is essential to research and compare their services, rates, and reputation. Look for reviews from other trucking businesses and drivers to gauge the quality of their services. You can also ask for recommendations from other industry professionals or check with your insurance provider for recommendations.

Some dispatching companies that are well-known and have a good reputation include Truckstop.com, DAT Solutions, and 123Loadboard. However, it is important to note that the best dispatching company for your business will depend on your specific needs, preferences, and budget.

Factoring Companies

you may have heard of factoring companies and wondered what their role is in your business. Factoring companies are financial institutions that provide a type of financing called freight factoring, which is specifically designed for the trucking industry. Factoring companies purchase your unpaid invoices and provide you with immediate cash, allowing you to manage your cash flow and maintain your operations without having to wait for your customers to pay.

The process of connecting and contacting factoring companies is relatively straightforward. You can conduct an online search using keywords such as "freight factoring companies" or "truck factoring companies" to find a list of companies that offer these services. You can also check with industry associations such as the American Trucking Associations (ATA) or the Owner-Operator Independent Drivers Association (OOIDA) for recommendations.

When choosing a factoring company, it is important to consider their rates, terms, and reputation. You should research and compare several companies to find the best fit for your business. Once you have identified a company that you would like to work with, you will need to provide them with basic information about your business, such as your average invoice size and volume, and your customers' payment history.

Factoring companies are essential to your trucking business because they can help you to manage your cash flow and maintain your operations. They provide you with immediate cash for your unpaid invoices, which can help you to cover expenses such as fuel, repairs, and driver wages. Factoring companies also handle the collections process, saving you time and resources, and reducing the risk of non-payment or late payment by your customers.

Locating Factoring Companies

There are several ways to locate and contact factoring companies. One way is to conduct an online search using keywords such as "freight factoring companies" or "truck factoring companies." This search will provide you with a list of companies that offer factoring services for the trucking industry.

Another way is to check with industry associations such as the American Trucking Associations (ATA) or the Owner-Operator Independent Drivers Association (OOIDA). These associations often have directories of factoring companies that specialize in providing services to the trucking industry.

When choosing a factoring company, it is important to research and compare their rates, terms, and reputation. Look for reviews from other trucking businesses to gauge the quality of their services. You can also ask for recommendations from other industry professionals or check with your insurance provider for recommendations.

Some factoring companies that are well-known and have a good reputation include Triumph Business Capital, TBS Factoring Service, and OTR Capital. However, it is important to note that the best factoring company for your business will depend on your specific needs, preferences, and budget.

Chapter Seven

Step 7: The Wrap Up

I am thrilled to introduce you to this book, and I hope it will be an invaluable guide and reference as you start your box truck business. This book drew on my personal experiences to provide answers to some of the most pressing questions that new entrepreneurs might have as they embark on their box truck journey.

My goal was to give you a fast-track guide that will help you avoid some of the common pitfalls that new box truck business owners face. Whether you're just starting out or you're looking to grow your existing business, this book is packed with practical advice that you can put into action right away.

I want you to know that starting a box truck business might not be the easiest venture, and you might face a few challenges along the way. However, I believe that with determination and hard work, you can overcome any obstacle that comes your way. The first 90 days might be the toughest, but please do not give up. Stay focused, remain on course, and continue to push through.

When I started my box truck business, I made a few mistakes, but I also learned a lot from those mistakes. In just 60 days, I made $65,000 over the road. While this might not seem like a lot, it was a significant learning curve for me, and it gave me the opportunity to familiarize myself with the box truck game and the rules of the road. Many companies might say that they don't want to work with you until you have spent at least 90 days on the road, but with time, you will become better at the job, and you will start making really good money. It's important to keep in mind that the cost per mile that companies offer is negotiable, so don't be afraid to negotiate. With the right approach and a little patience, box trucking can pay off in a big way.

As someone who has been in your shoes, I understand how daunting it can be to start a box truck business. That's why I created this book, to help you feel supported and motivated throughout your journey. I hope that the insights shared in this book will help you gain confidence and set you on a path to success. Thank you for choosing this book as your guide, and I wish you all the best on your box truck journey.

Chapter Eight

One Last Thing

T hank you once again for taking the time to read my book. If you have found it enjoyable or beneficial, I would greatly appreciate it if you could spare a few moments to write a brief review on Amazon Kindle. Your support means a lot to me, and it truly makes a difference. I genuinely value your feedback as it enables me to grow and enhance my work in the future. Thank you once more for your time and consideration.

Made in the USA
Monee, IL
01 November 2024